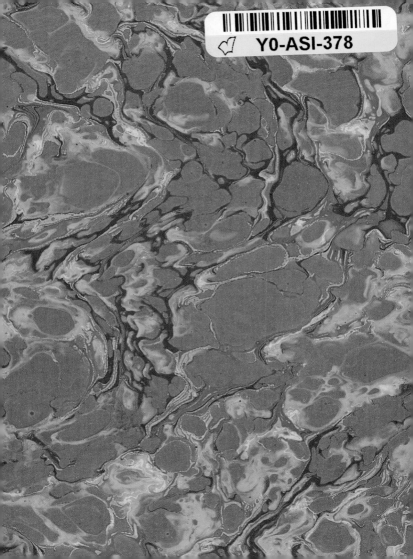

THE LITTLE
CAT VET
Book

ELIZABETH MARTYN
DAVID TAYLOR

DK

DORLING KINDERSLEY
London · New York · Stuttgart

A DORLING KINDERSLEY BOOK

PROJECT EDITOR Candida Ross-Macdonald

DESIGNER Camilla Fox

MANAGING EDITOR Krystyna Mayer

MANAGING ART EDITOR Derek Coombes

PRODUCTION Lauren Britton

First American Edition 1993
10 9 8 7 6 5 4 3 2 1

Published in Great Britain by Dorling Kindersley Limited.
Distributed by Houghton Mifflin Company, Boston.

ISBN 1-56458-264-7
Library of Congress Catalog Card Number 92-56496

Reproduced by Colourscan, Singapore
Printed and bound in Hong Kong by Imago

CONTENTS

ESSENTIAL

Cat

CARE

How to choose your pet and maintain it in the peak of good health.

CHOOSING A KITTEN

With luck, you and your new pet will spend many happy years together, so it makes sense to take your time and choose a kitten that is in the peak of health. Always go to either a reputable breeder or a humane society for a kitten. Avoid any pet shops where the animals are kept in cramped conditions, because young cats will pick up infections very readily. A breeder may let you return a pedigree kitten that falls ill soon after purchase.

In Top Shape
Watch the litter at play. Choose a kitten that is bright and enquiring: a shy one that hangs back may be weak or sick. Handle the kitten gently: it should respond happily to being picked up and fondled by humans.

WHICH SEX?

Whether you choose a male or a female makes little difference if you have your kitten neutered or spayed. There are differences, however, between entire toms and queens. Males tend to be more active and demand attention, but do not tolerate as much handling as females. They defend larger territories, and spray to mark them. Females roam and fight less, but while in season they may call all the local toms to your door.

SMALL BEGINNINGS

All kittens are adorable, but remember that they will change as they grow up.

SPOT THE DIFFERENCE

With tiny kittens this is not as easy as it sounds. Look below the tail. The anal opening is at the top, and on a female (far left) the vulva is immediately below it, so close that the two may look as though they are linked. On a male kitten (near left) the developing testicles can be seen as a dark patch below the anus, and the penis is below these.

CHECKING HEALTH

A quick all-over physical should pick up any obvious signs of malaise. Make sure that the kitten is lively and bouncy and can run and jump with ease. Examine your preferred kitten carefully before you say yes, following the pointers here. Don't separate a kitten from its mother before it is 10 to 12 weeks old, and make sure that it has been vaccinated against feline influenza and enteritis before you allow it out of doors. Regular boosters will be essential to maintain your cat's immunity.

CHECKS FOR GOOD HEALTH

1 *The kitten's teeth should be strong and white, the breath sweet-smelling, and the gums pink and healthy.*

2 *Look for clear, sparkling eyes with no sign of discharge or cloudiness. The third eyelid should not be visible.*

3 Gently check inside the ears for any discharge. Does the kitten scratch a lot? If so, it could indicate the presence of ear mites.

4 A slightly rounded tummy is normal in a kitten, but more pronounced distension may be a sign of roundworms.

5 The coat should have a glossy sheen and feel smooth and soft. Examine the skin for the black flecks that indicate fleas.

6 Take a look under the tail: the area should be clean, with no telltale signs of discharge or evidence of an upset stomach.

CARING FOR CLAWS

When "sharpening" its claws on a tree – or, worse, the sofa – your cat is actually scraping off a dead outer layer to reveal the new, sharp claw. Cats also use their teeth to do this. A cat's hindpaws have four clawed toes, its forepaws five, used to scratch itself, climb, grip, and deal with prey.

Think very carefully before declawing a cat. It is a traumatic step. Without claws a cat cannot climb, defend itself, or save itself when in danger of falling, and cannot tackle an excruciating itch.

Keeping in Trim

Cats that go outside regularly wear their claws down on hard surfaces and trees. Older cats and housebound felines should have their claws clipped regularly; if left to grow, the claws may curve back and dig into the paw.

Hold the cat's paw firmly and squeeze gently until the claws are exposed. Look at the claws and check for damage. A cat that comes home with several broken claws may have been involved in an accident, and should be given an overall check.

2 Carefully cut off the white tip of each claw, taking care to avoid the pink "quick" (see below). Trim the claws with special guillotine clippers, as here, or sharp nail clippers. Do not use scissors, because they could easily slip.

How Much to Trim

Look closely at a claw and you will see the pink "quick" inside it. This is living tissue, and cutting into it will cause bleeding and pain. If in doubt, trim less rather than more, or ask your vet to give you a demonstration before you tackle the job.

LOOKING AFTER TEETH

Kittens, like human babies, are born without teeth. Milk teeth start to appear at around three weeks, when a kitten first tastes solid food. These baby teeth are soon shed and replaced, and a cat has thirty adult teeth by the time it is six months old. At the front of the mouth are small incisors, used for delicate nibbling. On either side of these are long, sharp canines, designed for killing prey and tearing meat, and at the back of the mouth are strong premolars and molars, used for cutting, gripping, and crunching bones.

Sharp Tongue

As well as all those teeth, the cat has a tongue covered with fine, hard hooks, called papillae, that act rather like a set of extra small teeth. They make a rough surface, useful for licking meat off bones and grooming dead hair from the cat's coat.

Open the mouth carefully, pressing the jaws gently with your fingers. Check that the teeth look healthy and that the gums are pink and firm.

2 Introduce toothbrushing by lightly stroking the gums with a cotton swab. Apply a dot of pet toothpaste to your cat's lips as a flavor sample.

3 After a week or two, move on to proper brushing. Use a special, small-headed toothbrush from a pet shop, with a little pet toothpaste or salt water. Regular brushing will prevent tartar build-up, which can give gum problems in older cats. Dry foods in the diet to crunch, and chunks of meat to tear, also help to keep tartar at bay.

CARING FOR EYES AND EARS

The cat relies heavily on its eyes and ears, those super-sensitive receptors that enable it to be so aware of its surroundings. The eye is protected by an inner eyelid, the haw or nictitating membrane, which helps to deflect glare and keep the eyeball lubricated. Usually invisible, it may appear if a cat is unwell. Cat's eyes are very large in proportion to the face, giving them a stare designed to terrify enemies.

WELL **W**ASHED
Cats use paw power to keep the outsides of their ears meticulously clean, but are unable to remove dirt and wax from the insides. The large, pointed ear is designed to trap and channel the slightest sound.

Cleaning a Cat's Eyes

1 Check that there is no sign of discharge. Longhaired cats may have stains at the corners of the eyes that should be wiped away. Use a cotton ball moistened with warm water or baby oil.

2 Use a fresh cotton ball or swab for each eye, and wipe very gently to cleanse the surrounding fur. Make sure that you avoid the eyeball itself. Pat dry with a clean tissue.

Cleaning a Cat's Ears

The feline ear is delicate, so never be tempted to probe inside. Check first for any problems: dark wax indicates ear mites, which need treatment by a vet. Using a cotton ball moistened with water or baby oil, carefully remove dirt or wax from the insides of the ear flaps with a circular movement.

DEALING WITH FLEAS

Most cats that roam out of doors pick fleas up in the summer months. If not treated swiftly, they can all too easily reach epidemic proportions. If you suspect that your cat has fleas, check by parting the fur down to the skin and looking for black flecks. You may also spot the tiny, reddish brown insects themselves, scurrying for cover. Fleas most often lurk behind the ears, on the back of the neck, between the shoulder blades, and around the base of the tail. They can cause an itchy rash as well as bites. Seek veterinary help for this.

First Sign
Constant or frenzied scratching is a certain indication of the presence of fleas.

PEST CONTROL

Fleas lay eggs in carpets and in upholstered furniture, and a new crop appears in the house after a two-week incubation period. Fleas flourish in warm weather and centrally heated homes. Vacuum frequently to remove any eggs and fleas from your carpets, and empty the vacuum cleaner every time. Household insecticide sprays are available, and these should be used in suspect areas. Keep your cat's bedding scrupulously clean, and pay special attention to any spots where puss sleeps.

PREVENTION (above)
Flea collars release insecticide, and are effective for around three months. These collars can irritate the skin, so check them regularly.

. . . AND CURE (left)
Treat fleas with powders or sprays. Remember that the noise of a spray frightens some cats.

NUTRITION

An average adult cat needs three-quarters to a whole can of food per day, spread over one or two meals. Cats can live quite happily and healthily on a diet of ready-prepared food, but if you prefer to you can cook fresh food yourself. Choose lean cuts of meat or chicken, and cook them in stock or water. Most cats enjoy fish, but be extra careful to remove all bones. All food should be allowed to cool before serving; cats are very sensitive to the temperature of food, and will refuse anything that is too hot.

CANNED FOODS
Take canned food from the refrigerator 15 minutes before serving, and remove any uneaten remains within half an hour of mealtime.

GREEN NIBBLES
All cats appreciate a little greenery to nibble on. If your cat does not go out of doors, you can grow your own grass from seed in a pot kept especially for your pet.

Dietary Dos and Don'ts

Some cats cannot tolerate cow's milk. Fresh water should always be available, although your cat may not seem to drink a great deal.

Add bulk with cooked rice, pasta, or potato, but not too much. Dried food is good for teeth, but should not form the whole diet.

Some cats like egg. If yours does, serve scrambled egg – never give raw egg. Limit scraps and between-meal snacks.

Give your cat small amounts of raw or cooked vegetables for extra vitamins and minerals. Remember, however, that cats are carnivores, and cannot survive on a vegetarian diet.

Portly Puss

A fat cat may suffer health problems and could die young. If your cat is overweight, ask your vet whether there is a medical reason. If there is not, you must reduce food consumption – your vet will be able to advise on a balanced reducing diet. Check that your cat is not being fed elsewhere or supplementing your provisions by hunting.

WHEN TO VISIT THE VET

Keep a careful eye on your cat, so that symptoms of
illness are spotted – and treated – early on.

Body, Coat, and Skin
*Frantic scratching indicates
fleas or ticks. Use a spray
or powder and buy a flea
collar. See the vet for
anything other than minor
scratches, especially if bald
patches, blisters, or sores appear.
Investigate under the fur if the cat
flinches when handled and seek
advice on any lumps under the skin.
Consult a vet immediately if your
cat has difficulty walking or jumping.*

Appetite
*Seek help if listlessness and loss of
appetite, vomiting, or diarrhea
continue beyond 24 hours. Keep an
eye out for excessive thirst, urination
problems, and sudden weight changes.*

Ears, Nose, and Eyes

Constant head-shaking or ear-scratching indicate ear mites: your vet can prescribe drops for these. Seek veterinary advice if puss develops a cough. Sneezes or snuffles, or bleary, reddened, or runny eyes might indicate cat flu: isolate your cat and see the vet immediately. If the inner eyelid covers part of the eye, as left, see the vet immediately.

You and Your Vet

All vets are trained to treat cats, but it is best to choose one who specializes in small pets. Ask other cat owners in the area for recommendations, and register your cat with a vet from kittenhood. Some animal charities provide subsidized treatment, if the cost of veterinary care is a problem. If you suspect that your cat is unwell, consult a vet as soon as possible. Attempting to diagnose and treat a problem yourself can do more harm than good.

Transporting Your Cat

As a cat owner you will need some means of transporting your pet, even if the only trips you make are the annual visits to the vet's office for booster vaccinations. If your cat needs veterinary attention after being involved in an accident, move it as little as possible in case it has internal injuries. It may be difficult to put an injured cat into its usual carrier, and if someone else is available to drive, it is sometimes easier to wrap the cat gently but securely in a towel and carry it in your lap.

What to Take
For all but the shortest trips, take food and water, dishes, and an old blanket or towel for lining the carrier.

Basket Case

A nervous cat can "hide" in a wicker carrier, while a bolder one can look out and watch the world going by. This kind of carrier is difficult to clean thoroughly, however, and a very determined cat may be able to bite or claw an escape route.

Wired Up

Open-mesh carriers are escape proof, simple to clean, and provide excellent ventilation. A generous lining of towels or newspaper provides a cozy and accident-proof bed to lie on.

Boxed In

Cardboard carriers are cheap, but only suitable for short trips or emergencies.

FAMILY
Cats

*Advice on the breeding
and care of kittens,
and on what to do
to avoid them.*

KITTENING

A feline pregnancy lasts on average about nine weeks. After three or four weeks of gestation a veterinary examination will tell you whether your cat is pregnant. By six weeks she will start to grow noticeably plumper, and her nipples will become pinker and more prominent. During pregnancy a queen's normal weight increases by one-quarter to one-third. A pregnant female needs a good, nourishing diet, increased to about one-third more food than usual in the latter half of gestation. She should be allowed to climb and play as usual, although she may slow down as the pregnancy progresses.

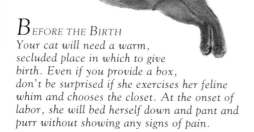

Before the Birth
Your cat will need a warm,
secluded place in which to give
birth. Even if you provide a box,
don't be surprised if she exercises her feline
whim and chooses the closet. At the onset of
labor, she will bed herself down and pant and
purr without showing any signs of pain.

As Birth Approaches

Introduce the mother to her maternity bed – a box lined with newspaper, with one side removed, is ideal – in good time, and encourage her to sleep in it.

Keep the mother indoors for the last couple of days before the kittens are due, in case she hides herself away, and remember that kittens are often born at night.

An expectant queen may refuse her food or vomit shortly before she goes into labor.

Baby Talk

At 12 hours, kittens are blind and deaf. Their sense of smell, already well developed, helps them to keep track of mom.

Mum's the Word

Labor may take some hours. If the mother seems to be tiring, offer milk or a little light food. Most cats deliver their kittens without human intervention. Keep an eye on your pet, but don't interfere unless you have to. Call a vet if nothing has happened within 30 minutes of your cat starting to strain, or if a kitten is stuck.

POSTNATAL CARE

Kittens begin to suckle shortly after birth, and the maternal bond is forged in the first few days. After this, mother and kittens recognize each other by smell and voice. A nursing mother should be given extra food in her diet until the kittens are weaned.

CARRYING KITTENS

A new mother will stand guard over her kittens and will try not to leave them for the first few days. If a kitten crawls away, its mother will carry it to safety, gripping it gently but firmly by the scruff of its neck.

NEARLY NEW

Only a few days old, these kittens can already purr and will hiss if alarmed. Like babies, young cats spend their early days just eating and sleeping. After a meal kittens snuggle up for a snooze, staying close together for mutual warmth and safety.

Hand Rearing

If a mother cat cannot feed all of her young, or if she rejects one of them, it is possible to raise kittens by hand on artificial milk from a vet or a pet shop. Initially, feeding is needed every two hours, and kittens can be fed with a bottle or, if they are very weak, a plastic dropper. Seek veterinary advice on the general care of very young kittens.

A Loving Lick

. mother cat will often lick her .ttens. When they are newborn, .e licks them to clean them and .imulate their circulation. For .e first few weeks, while the kittens feed only on milk, she licks under their tails to stimulate excretion. Even when kittens are older and more independent, they are treated to a maternal wash.

CARE OF YOUNG KITTENS

You may be longing to get acquainted with the latest
additions to the household, but newborn kittens
should be handled as little as possible until they have
formed the all-important bond of scent with their
mother. When you do pick kittens up, handle their
fragile bodies with care, and never squeeze them.
Supervise children, who will want to play with kittens,
but often don't realize how
delicate they are.

WEIGH IN
A kitten's weight
doubles in its
first week of life,
and continues
to increase
rapidly for
two months.

Early Learning

Start litter training when kittens are three to four weeks old. Find a quiet corner for the tray, and pop the kittens in after every meal. They should soon get the idea, although some early mishaps are unfortunately inevitable.

Starting on Solids

Introduce solids into the kittens' diet when they are three to four weeks old.

Offer small amounts four to six times a day at first, and move to fewer larger meals. Aim to have the kittens fully weaned by eight weeks.

❧ Give cooked, chopped meat or poultry, or canned kitten food. Many kittens also enjoy scrambled eggs or baby cereals mixed with milk.

❧ Cat milk substitute provides nourishment and encourages kittens to drink.

Drinking Partners

Give kittens plenty of fresh water to drink once they start on solid foods.

NEUTERING

Male cats have a reputation for being less loving and affectionate than their female counterparts, but this is only true of unneutered toms. Neutered toms make docile and delightful pets. They are unlikely to roam too far afield and are far less aggressive towards other cats than entire males – characteristics that also make them and their owners more popular with the neighbors. The neutering operation can be carried out at any age, but ideally it should be performed when the cat is around six months old. The procedure of removing the testes is very simple, and is carried out under general anaesthetic. No special aftercare is needed, and your pet should show no ill effects.

TRADEMARK
An unneutered tom leaves his mark around his territory - indoors and out – by spraying it with strong-smelling urine. The earlier a male cat is castrated, the less likely he is to develop this antisocial habit.

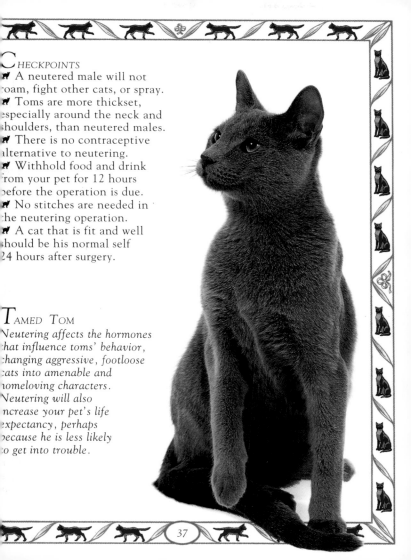

CHECKPOINTS

🐈 A neutered male will not roam, fight other cats, or spray.

🐈 Toms are more thickset, especially around the neck and shoulders, than neutered males.

🐈 There is no contraceptive alternative to neutering.

🐈 Withhold food and drink from your pet for 12 hours before the operation is due.

🐈 No stitches are needed in the neutering operation.

🐈 A cat that is fit and well should be his normal self 24 hours after surgery.

TAMED TOM

Neutering affects the hormones that influence toms' behavior, changing aggressive, footloose cats into amenable and homeloving characters. Neutering will also increase your pet's life expectancy, perhaps because he is less likely to get into trouble.

SPAYING

You may have great plans to breed from your pedigree queen, but find out exactly what is involved first. The process can be both expensive, involving veterinary and stud fees, and time-consuming, since both mother and kittens will need good care. Breeding from a non-pedigree female is not advisable, because far too many unwanted cats are born every year. It is sometimes said that a cat should be allowed to have one litter before being spayed, but there is no advantage to this. The operation is simple and safe: the womb and both ovaries are removed under general anesthetic. A small area around the incision is shaved, and your cat should be discouraged from pulling at the stitches. Recovery is quick, and the coat soon grows back to cover the tiny scar.

*F*AST BREEDER
With three or four kittens in a litter, the feline population grows readily if left unchecked.

CHECKPOINTS

♥ There is no visible
difference between a spayed cat
and a queen, but a spayed
female will not go into heat or
"call" for a mate.

♥ A feline contraceptive pill is
available for female cats if
surgery is unsuitable.

♥ Withhold food and drink for
12 hours before the operation.

♥ Your pet may be a little less
active than usual for a couple
of days after spaying.

♥ The stitches may dissolve by
themselves, or they may need
to be removed by a vet a
week or so after surgery.

EARLY STARTERS

*A female cat should
be spayed when she
is between four and
five months of age.
She may appear
little more than a
kitten herself, but
queens come into
heat for the first
time when they are
just six months old.*

MEDICAL
CARE FOR
Cats

*Restraining and examining
a cat, administering
medication, and caring for
a sick cat at home.*

RESTRAINING A CAT

It will be necessary to restrain your cat to allow an examination, or to administer pills, liquid medicines, or eye or ear drops. Many cats are very well behaved in these circumstances, provided that their owners give them plenty of reassurance by stroking them and talking while holding them gently but firmly. Never use excessive force: this could make a reluctant cat struggle more and might even cause injury. Wrapping in a towel is a good restraint method to use at home if your cat does not like to take medicine.

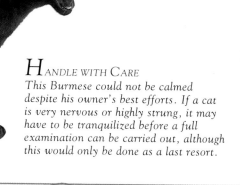

Handle with Care
This Burmese could not be calmed despite his owner's best efforts. If a cat is very nervous or highly strung, it may have to be tranquilized before a full examination can be carried out, although this would only be done as a last resort.

Mild Restraint

Restraining a Difficult Cat

Hold the front legs gently in your hands and restrain the body with your forearms.

Grasp the scruff with one hand, with the arm along the back, and hold the front legs in the other.

Wrapping a Cat in a Towel

Grasp the scruff and place the cat on a towel, which should kept hidden beforehand.

2 Still holding the scruff, wrap the cat, taking care to trap the paws inside the towel.

Examining a Cat

A healthy cat is active, interested, and alert. The most obvious indicators of health problems are changes in your pet's behavior, such as listlessness an loss of appetite. A sick cat often does not show any such symptoms, however, and without checks you ma not notice that something is wrong. The health checks that you make when first choosing a kitten (*see pages 12–13*) should be carried out regularly, so that you spot any changes in condition early on, and checks of the pulse, temperature, and breathing should be made if you think there is anything amiss.

VITAL SIGNS
A sick cat often loses interest in life and hides away. A chan in behavior may indicat problems.

CHECKING THE ESSENTIALS

Choose a time when your cat is relaxed, maybe after grooming, to make your checks. Put it on a raised surface where you can examine it easily. Talk to it reassuringly as you look for any evidence of ill health. If all is well, your cat should respond happily to being handled, and will show no signs of distress or discomfort. With a little patience and practice, taking your pet's temperature and pulse and checking its breathing should not present you with any problems.

1 Feel the pulse in the groin. The normal rate for a cat is 110 to 140 beats per minute.

2 A vet checks breathing with a stethoscope. Listen for a labored sound, wheezing, coughing, or change in voice.

3 Smear the thermometer with petroleum jelly, shake, and insert under tail for one minute. Normal temperature is 38 to 39°.

ADMINISTERING MEDICINE

Many common feline complaints are treated with tablets, and it is useful for an owner to acquire the trick of giving both pills and liquids with the least possible fuss. Some cats are calm and obliging and will swallow pills readily, allowing their owners to give medications singlehanded. Other cats, however, are less compliant, and with these cats it is a good idea to have some assistance on hand.

Sneaky Snack
It may be worth trying to wrap pills in food if your cat resists other methods, but be vigilant. Those super-sensitive feline senses of smell and taste can usually detect hidden tablets, and a clever cat pretends to swallow, then spits out the offending item when its owner's back is turned.

Giving Tablets

1 If necessary, enlist a helper to hold the cat's body. Tilt the head back, covering the ears but avoiding the sensitive whiskers, and press gently on the jaws to open the mouth.

2 Pop the pill into the cat's mouth, getting it as far back as possible. Quickly close the mouth, and stroke the throat gently to encourage salivation until you feel the cat swallow.

Giving Liquids

To give liquids to a placid cat, use a spoon and proceed slowly. Flex the head back gently and press on the jaws to open the mouth. Give medicine gradually, so that it runs down the tongue, and pause to let the cat swallow after every few drops. With a difficult cat, use a plastic syringe, squeezing the medicine slowly into the corner of the mouth.

TREATING EYE PROBLEMS

Eyes are vulnerable, and may be scratched in a fight or
when a cat pushes through brambles. Cats can also
contract eye infections. Signs of problems include
excessive blinking, watering or discharge from the eye,
partial or complete closure of the lid, inflammation or
swelling, cloudiness, or a change in color. If the inner
eyelid is damaged or infected, it may appear inflamed
and protrude across the eye. The cat may paw at the
eye, or show signs of blindness such as walking into
objects or losing
coordination. Always
seek veterinary help
immediately.

Wide Eyed

*Eyes are delicate. Do not apply
medication without a vet's
prescription, and never use eye
drops meant for humans
on a cat. If you
notice signs of
infection, bathe the
eyes gently with
warm water and
consult a vet.*

Cradling the head in your hands, hold the tube parallel the eye – never point it into the e. Squeeze the tube, drawing a ead of ointment across the eye.

2 Close the eye gently and hold it shut for a few seconds so that the ointment can dissolve and spread. Talk to the cat quietly and soothingly.

ADMINISTERING EYE DROPS

Put your free hand under the cat's chin, and the hand holding the bottle or dropper on the back of its head. Tilt the head back and sideways, bringing the eye to be treated uppermost. Keep the applicator away from the eye. Apply drops in the outer corner of the eye and let them flow across the eyeball. Close the eye and hold it shut for a few seconds.

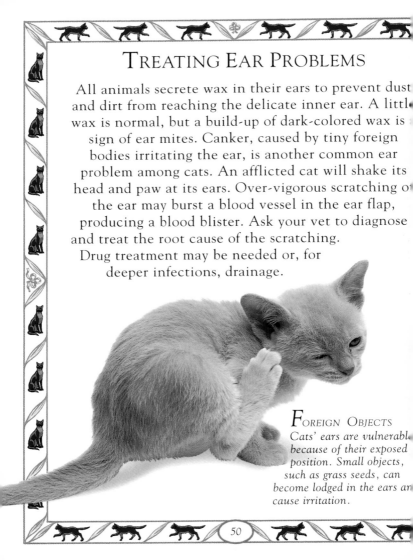

TREATING EAR PROBLEMS

All animals secrete wax in their ears to prevent dust and dirt from reaching the delicate inner ear. A little wax is normal, but a build-up of dark-colored wax is a sign of ear mites. Canker, caused by tiny foreign bodies irritating the ear, is another common ear problem among cats. An afflicted cat will shake its head and paw at its ears. Over-vigorous scratching of the ear may burst a blood vessel in the ear flap, producing a blood blister. Ask your vet to diagnose and treat the root cause of the scratching. Drug treatment may be needed or, for deeper infections, drainage.

*F*OREIGN OBJECTS
Cats' ears are vulnerable because of their exposed position. Small objects, such as grass seeds, can become lodged in the ears and cause irritation.

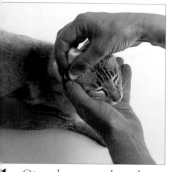

1 Open the ear gently and cleanse inside the flap with a cotton swab, moistened with warm water or olive oil. Never probe inside the ear with the bud.

2 Have the medication at body temperature. Apply the correct dose to each ear. Do not poke the dropper into the ear canal: let the drops fall into it.

3 Using your thumbs, massage the base of the ear with gentle pressure for several minutes, to encourage the drops to spread. When released, the cat will shake its head from side to side. This may loosen softened debris in the ear, which can then be carefully wiped away. Only remove what is readily accessible: do not probe into the ear canal, because you can easily damage the delicate organs within.

NURSING A SICK CAT

A cat that is ill or recuperating after an operation
may need special care. Nursing is best done at home,
by people familiar with the cat. Provide a warm bed,
perhaps in a newspaper-lined box, to protect the
patient from drafts. Position a litter box nearby, and
keep the entire area scrupulously clean. A sick cat
should not be allowed to go outside. Groom the cat
gently, cleansing the face with warm water if there is
any discharge from the eyes, nose, or mouth.

WARM AS TOAST
*A tepid hot-water bottle under
a blanket makes a cozy bed.
Never use an uncovered bottle.*

Well Dressed

An injured cat may need bandaging. This is best done by a vet for all but very minor wounds. Check the dressing regularly to see that it does not become too tight or work loose. Cats often try to remove dressings and may have to be restrained with a "ruff" collar.

Tempting Morsels

Sick cats often lose their appetites. Offer a little of a favorite food, lukewarm in a clean bowl. You may have to spoonfeed liquids, dropping them into the mouth slowly. If this fails, use a plastic dropper inserted in a corner of the mouth.

Nursing Notes

🐈 Keep a sick cat in a quiet, well-ventilated, but draft-free room. Keep any strangers away.

🐈 Provide small meals at regular intervals, and make sure that your cat always has fresh drinking water available.

🐈 Avoid loud noises that might startle the patient.

🐈 Avoid disinfectants or antiseptics containing phenol or iodine. Dilute hydrogen peroxide, available from pharmacies and used according to directions, is a safe cleaning agent.

MY CAT'S HEALTH RECORD

Name . . . .

Date of birth . . . . Sex . . . .

Breed . . . .

First vaccination . . . .

Booster vaccination . . . .

Other vaccinations . . . .

. . . .

Date of spaying/neutering . . . .

Worming tablets given. . . . .

Flea preparations used. . . . .

Dietary likes and dislikes . . . .

. . . .

Allergies . . . .

. . . .

Any special health needs . . . .

. . . .

Name and address of vet . . . .

. . . .

. . . .

Telephone number . . . .

Emergency telephone number . . . .

Illnesses (record date, diagnosis, and treatment) . . . .

. . . .

. . . .

. . . .

. . . .

. . . .

. . . .

. . . .

. . . .

Accidents (record date, cause, and treatment) . . . .

. . . .

. . . .

. . . .

A-Z OF HEALTH

A IS FOR ARTIFICIAL RESPIRATION

To revive a cat that has inhaled water, hold it securely by the hind legs and swing it vigorously (but not violently) down to expél water from the lungs. Do not try this method if the cat is unconscious or if its hind legs or back have been injured.

C IS FOR CLEANING

If a cat sprays indoors, clean the area immediately with a solution of vinegar and water. This old-fashioned remedy works well to remove any traces of scent, and discourage further spraying, but check the surface for color fastness before applying.

B IS FOR BLINDNESS

Many cats adapt surprisingly well to this disability, relying on their acute senses of smell and hearing instead. A blind cat must be kept indoors and taught where obstacles are. Don't move furniture; changes make life harder.

D IS FOR DESTRUCTIVE

A cat that habitually claws furniture or curtains, or chews wool, may be bored or lonely. Consider providing a feline companion.

E IS FOR ELECTRICITY

Some cats will chew electrical cables. Coat all your cables with nasty-tasting eucalyptus oil to discourage this, and provide chews and catnip toys as a distraction. Unplug appliances when they are not in use.

F IS FOR FASTIDIOUS

A cat may refuse to eat if the food bowls are too close to the litter box for its liking. Keep feeding and toilet areas completely separate.

G IS FOR GINGIVITIS

This inflammation of the gums causes a cat discomfort, especially when eating. It can also be a symptom of other ailments, so you should always seek veterinary advice.

H IS FOR HYGIENE

Wash and rinse both food and water bowls thoroughly after every meal. Keep your cat's bedding clean and launder or replace it frequently to prevent it being infested by fleas.

I IS FOR INSURANCE

Medical insurance is widely available and a wise investment. All vets' fees for accidents and illnesses can be covered, although fees for routine vaccinations and for neutering and spaying cannot.

J IS FOR JABS

Injections and vaccinations are usually given in the scruff of the neck and are virtually painless. Try to relax when you go to the vet's office. If you are worried, you cat will become anxious too, and the more tense it is, the more difficult it will be.

K IS FOR KIDNEYS

These are vulnerable, particularly in older cats. Watch for excessive thirst, increased production of urine, discomfort in urination, weight loss, and decline in condition. Seek treatment promptly.

L IS FOR LITTER BOXES

Keep the litter box in a quiet corner: your cat will appreciate the privacy. Some timid cats even prefer a covered box. Clean the litter box out frequently: this is especially important if more than one cat uses the box. For easier day-to-day cleaning, choose litter that forms clumps when soiled. You should replace the whole boxful with fresh litter at least once a week for hygiene. Wash the box out thoroughly each time that you change the litter.

M IS FOR MOLTING

This is a regular springtime event for almost all breeds of cat. If your cat sheds unusual amounts of hair outside the molting season, look for signs of skin problems, such as fleas or other parasites, or sore, broken, or lumpy skin. Your vet will be able to prescribe suitable treatments for these.

N IS FOR NERVOUS DISORDERS

These are most frequently the result of accidents in which the head or spine has been injured. If your cat staggers or stumbles, trembles violently, or cannot move at all, it may have been hurt even if there is no sign of external injury. You must seek immediate veterinary help.

O IS FOR OVEREATING

If your cat's appetite increases for more than two weeks, you should ask for veterinary advice. Internal parasites or a metabolic disorder are the most likely explanations.

P IS FOR PREGNANCY

If you think your cat may be expecting, look for a gradual increase in weight, increased color in the nipples, and a swollen belly. A vet can confirm the pregnancy and estimate the delivery date.

Q IS FOR QUARANTINE

These regulations are essential to protect rabies-free countries. Check the rules before you travel abroad with your cat.

R IS FOR REJECTION

An established cat may resent the introduction of a new kitten into the household and refuse to accept the newcomer. Proceed slowly and keep the two apart, allowing supervised meetings every day. If after three weeks there is no improvement, you may have to accept defeat and find a home for the kitten elsewhere.

S IS FOR STRESS

Cats may suffer stress following a change in routine, a change of location, or the loss of a valued companion. Symptoms include a reduced appetite, increased scratching of furniture, hair loss, and spraying. Establish and deal with the cause, and the symptoms should soon disappear.

T IS FOR TAIL
The Manx cat manages without a tail. However, if completely tailless (Rumpy) Manx cats breed, the genetic mutation usually results in the death of the kittens.

U IS FOR URINE
Spraying urine is a method of scent-marking associated with tom cats. Neutering male cats prevents the problem, although any cat – male or female, neutered or not – may spray occasionally when under stress.

V IS FOR VOMITING
Cats vomit easily, a protection against harmful substances. If your cat is vomiting continuously or repeatedly, however, seek veterinary advice.

W IS FOR WOOL
A few cats seem to enjoy munching on their owners' scarves and sweaters, a habit that may lead to intestinal problems. Keep tempting fabric items out of your cat's reach, and provide a constant supply of dry food, in addition to the cat's normal diet, to satisfy the feline impulse to snack.

X IS FOR XERCISE
Most cats will get plenty of healthy activity just from roaming around outside. If your cat must live its life indoors, make sure that it has a daily play session and is encouraged to run around by being given a variety of toys to chase.

Y IS FOR YARN
A ball of yarn makes a tempting toy, but it could be dangerous if your cat swallowed the end of it. Ping-pong balls and special toys made for cats are safer.

Z IS FOR ZINC
A mineral vital for growth, healing, and skin condition. Make sure that your cat gets enough by feeding cooked beef, lamb, liver, cheese, and – as a special treat – oysters!

INDEX

ACKNOWLEDGMENTS

Key: t=top, b=bottom

All photography by Steve Gorton and Tim Ridley except for:
Jane Burton: 8, 18, 32, 36, 38
Jane Burton/Bruce Coleman Ltd: 24t
Marc Henrie: 9, 11t, 14, 37, 39, 57
Dave King: 41, 59
Matthew Ward: 5, 25b, 53t

Design Assistance: Patrizio Semproni
Picture Research: Diana Morris
Illustration: Chris Forsey, Stephen Lings, Clive Spong

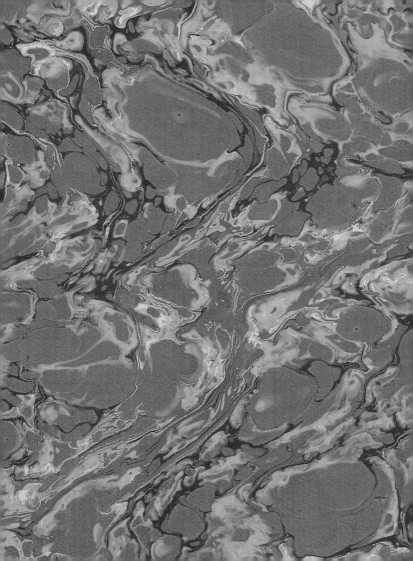